Ice Fight

Janice Pimm • Jon Stuart

Contents

Welcome to Micro World! .... page 2
The Ice Palace .... page 5
Fire and Ice .... page 13

This page is for an adult to read to you.

Welcome to Micro World!

Macro Marvel
(billionaire inventor)

Macro Marvel invented Micro World – a micro-sized theme park where you have to shrink to get in.

A computer called **CODE** controls Micro World and all the robots inside – MITEs and BITEs.

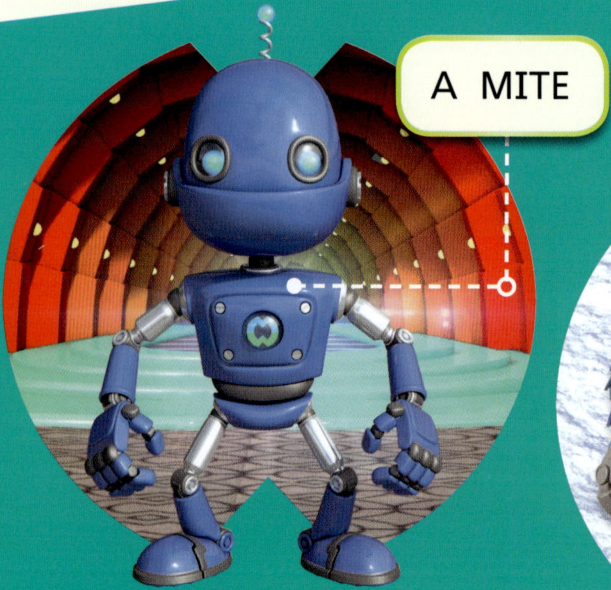

A MITE

A BITE

Disaster strikes!

CODE goes wrong on opening day.
CODE wants to shrink the world.

Macro Marvel is trapped inside the park …

This page is for an adult to read to you.

Enter Team X!

Four micro agents – **Max**, **Cat**, **Ant** and **Tiger** – are sent to rescue Macro Marvel and defeat CODE.

Mini Marvel joins Team X.

Mini Marvel
(Macro's daughter)

In the last book ...

- Max, Cat and Ant were riding on the Skyway when the Ice-BITE cut the cable!
- They plunged down the snowy slope.
- Mini and Tiger used the huskies to rescue Max, Cat and Ant.

**CODE key
(7 collected)**

You are in the Big Freeze zone.

Before you read

Sound checker
Say the sound.

g

Sound spotter
Blend the sounds.

| h | u | ge |

| m | a | g | i | c |

| d | a | n | g | er |

Tricky word

once

Into the zone

What do you think Team X, Mini and Rex will do next?

The Ice Palace

Team X, Mini and Rex were standing near the cliff. "Look what's over the edge!" said Cat.

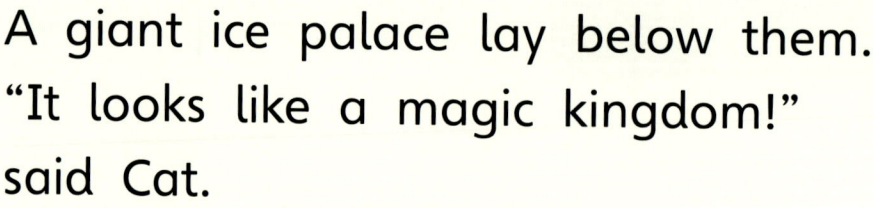

A giant ice palace lay below them.
"It looks like a magic kingdom!" said Cat.
"I bet the Ice-BITE hides there," said Mini. "I'll look on my Gizmo."

Ice Palace map

Enter the palace – home to the Ice-BITE. Once you get past the MITEs, don't get lost in the maze!

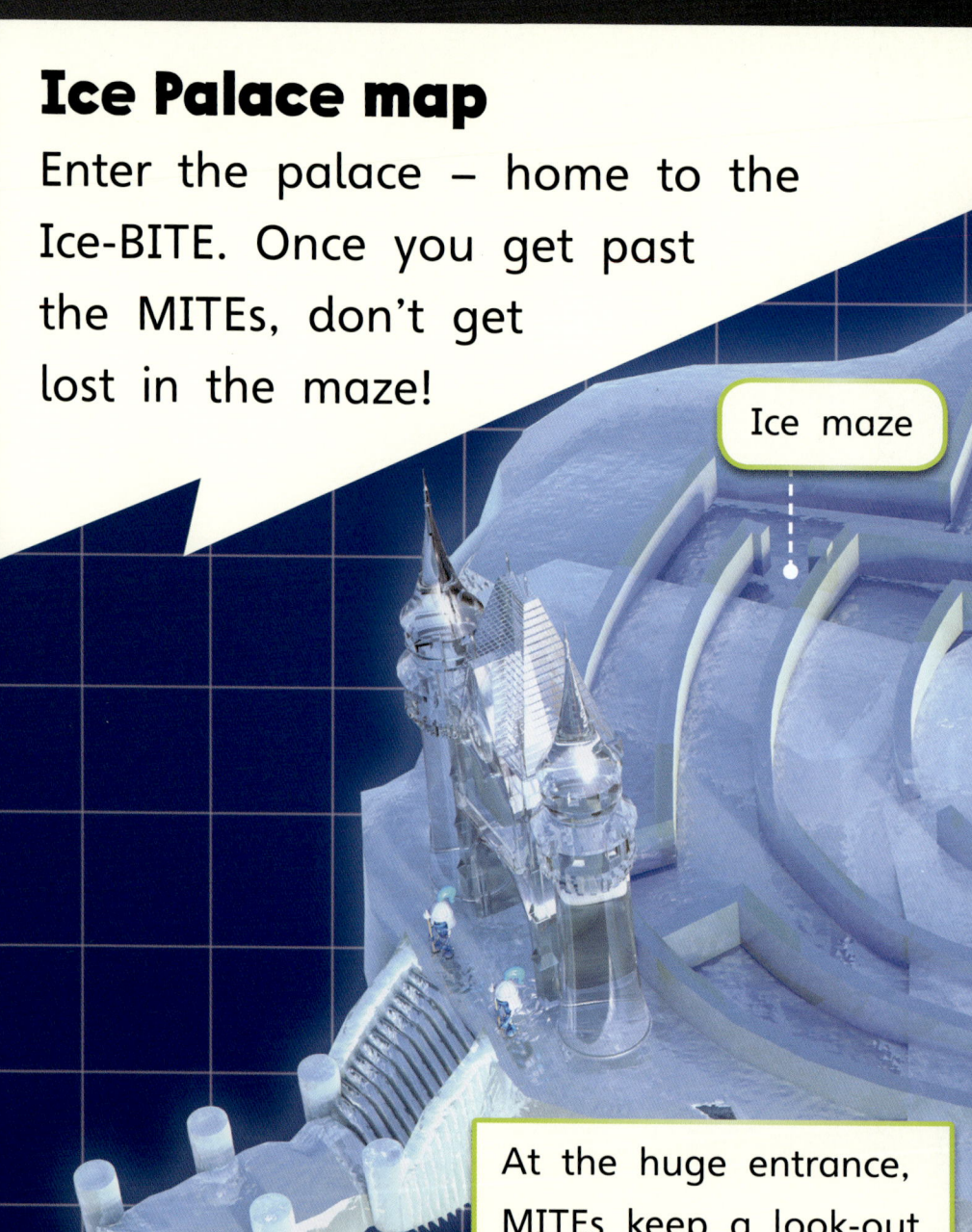

Ice maze

At the huge entrance, MITEs keep a look-out for danger.

"That's it! The CODE key is in the secret chamber," said Mini. "How will we get to the palace?" "We'll shrink and fly there in Hawkwing," said Max.

This page is for an adult to read with you.

Now you have read ...
The Ice Palace

Take a closer look
Answer these questions.

- Who do you think is the most excited?
- How does Mini know where the CODE key is hidden?
- How will Team X, Mini and Rex find their way through the ice maze?
- Why are MITEs guarding the entrance?

Thinking time
Cat said the ice palace looked like a magic kingdom. Why do you think she said that?

How can we get past the MITEs?

This page is for an adult to read with you.   This page is for an adult to read with you.

Before you read

Sound checker
Say the sound.

g

Sound spotter
Blend the sounds.

| g | i | a | n | t |

| e | n | er | g | y |

| g | e | n | t | l | y |

Tricky word
once

Into the zone
What must Max, Ant and Mini do to get the CODE key?

12

Fire and Ice

Max, Ant and Mini flew to the ice palace. Rex distracted the MITEs while Hawkwing flew inside.

Using the map on her Gizmo, Mini led the way through the ice maze.

Suddenly, with a giant roar, the Ice-BITE appeared! It began to shoot freeze rays at once.

Rex tried to shoot fire back. Instantly, the BITE froze the flames! "It's going to turn us into ice!" cried Max. "Run!"

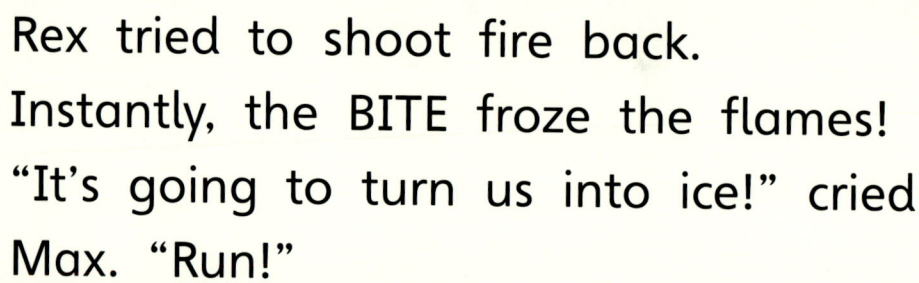

Ant bumped into a wall of ice. "We're trapped," he cried.

Max put on his power mitts and used all his energy to make a giant crack in the ice. Ant, Mini and Rex climbed through.

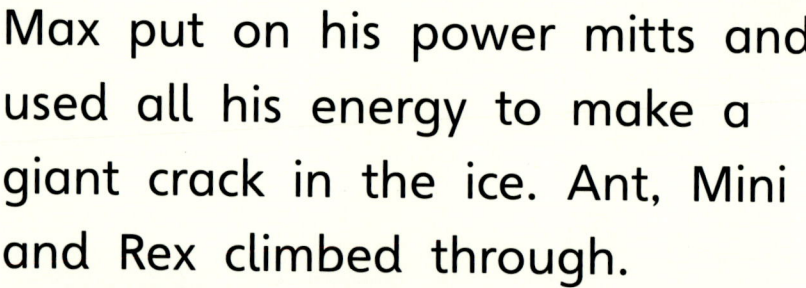

Suddenly, the Ice-BITE shot its freeze rays at Max!

"Look! The secret chamber," cried Ant.

"This is an emergency! We have to get the CODE key and rescue Max," said Mini.

The CODE key was lodged inside an ice cube. Rex breathed fire gently to melt the ice.

Quickly, Mini picked up the CODE key.

The Ice-BITE shut down. At once, Max started to melt!

They made their way to meet Cat and Tiger at the exit.
"I love this zone!" said Tiger.
"I don't," said Max. "I'm going somewhere to get warm!"

Now you have read ...
Fire and Ice

To get to the next zone we have to read the CODE words. Then the exit door will open. Can you help us read them?

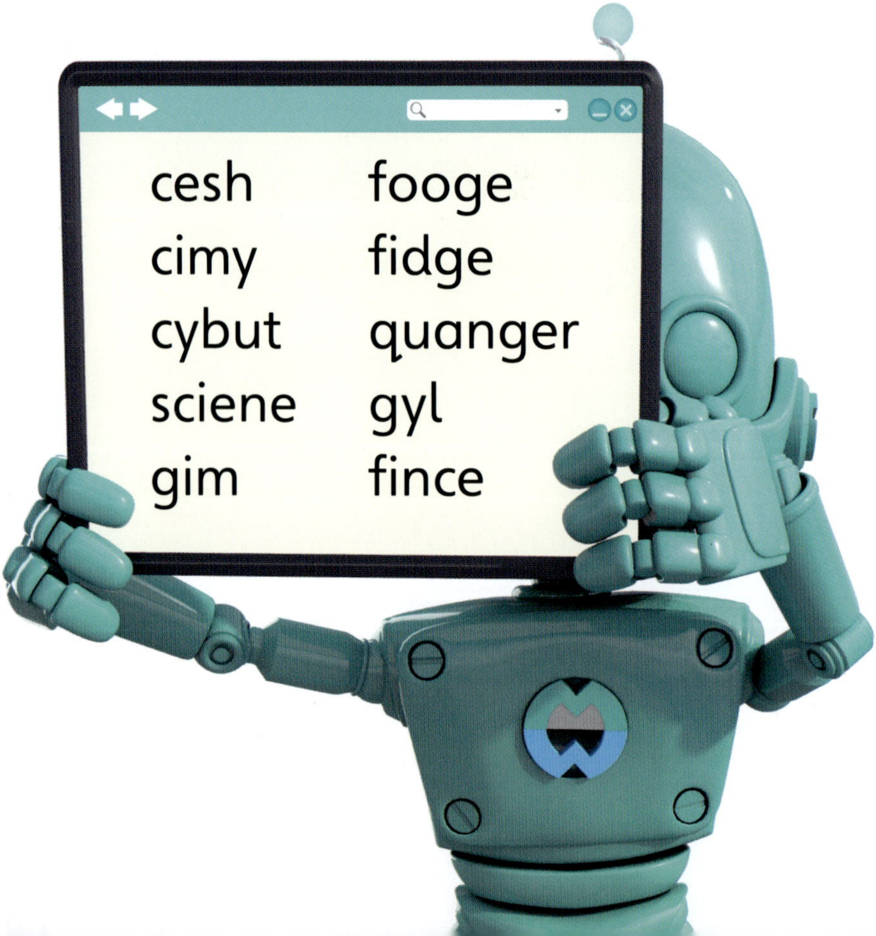

cesh   fooge
cimy   fidge
cybut   quanger
sciene gyl
gim   fince